VAl

CW00422443

a short
guide to good
**parenting**

little
book
series

First published 2008
Copyright © 2008
Reprinted 2010 and 2014
All rights reserved. No part of this publication
may be reproduced in any form without prior
permission from the publisher.

British Library Cataloguing in Publication Data.
Catalogue record for this book is available from
the British Library.

ISBN 978-1-906381-00-4

Published by Autumn House Limited,
Grantham, Lincolnshire.

Printed in China.

Bible versions used:
NLT = *New Living Translation*
NIV = *New International Version*
KJV = *King James Version*
NKJV = *New King James Version*

**Direct your children onto the right path, and when they are older, they will not leave it.**

Proverbs 22:6, NLT

# Parents need courage

It takes time. Don't give up after a few tries. Poor behaviour was not learned overnight, so new behaviour will not be learned overnight. It takes time to unlearn old behaviour patterns.

**You *can* change your behaviour and that of your child!**

**Commitment to the task is the key.**

# What sort of example are you?

A boy once wrote this to his mother and father: 'You parents start wars and set a terrible example regarding morals and honesty, yet you expect us to be angels. We are only copying you. Why don't you practise what you preach?'

# Changing parental habits

Changes in behaviour need to begin with us.

Behavioural psychology has discovered that when you break your habitual response to any given situation, your change can and will modify the entire situation. For example, if you respond differently to your child's behaviour (or misbehaviour), his behaviour will change.

# The perfect parent?

Perfection in parenting is an unattainable goal. Improvement, however, is realistic. Watch, then, for little improvements. Each small improvement is a step forward. So when you try a new method, and it works, be happy!

# Theory into practice

There was a psychologist who had six theories on rearing children and no children. He ended up with six children and no theories!

Take account of the fact that most of us have received absolutely no training in parenting. Given that state of affairs, we do a remarkable job.

# A parental guilt trip?

Guilt feelings do not produce good parents. The fact that you are studying to become a better parent shows that you truly care about your children.

So don't dwell on your failures, and don't reproach yourself when you fall back into old habits.

# Whose image?

*Children are a gift from the Lord;*
*    They are a reward from him.*
*Children born to a young man*
*    Are like arrows in a warrior's hands.*
*How joyful is the man whose quiver is full*
*of them!*
Psalm 127:3, 4, 5, NLT

**Will your child reflect the image
of God?**

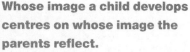

**Whose image a child develops
centres on whose image the
parents reflect.**

# Feelings
# of inferiority

Nearly everyone suffers from feelings of
inadequacy. We see evidence of this
mass-tragedy on every hand – in every
neighbourhood, church and school.

Although feelings of inadequacy are evident
in small children, they become particularly
apparent during adolescence.

Most teenagers are bitterly disappointed in
who they are, what they look like, and what
they are accomplishing.

# How self-image is acquired

People of every age face their own particular brand of inadequacy.

A child of 5 can tell how important he is to those around him.

Many adults face severe feelings of inferiority.

Senior citizens also feel that sting in a world that worships youth.

# Self-respect

In the West billions of men and women succumb annually to cardiovascular disease. However, there is a greater killer of human life that stalks the Earth.

A lack of self-respect plagues more people, cripples more lives, and renders useless more individuals than the world's greatest health problem.

# Your child's mental picture of himself is very important

How your child feels about himself will determine his success or failure in each of life's endeavours. How he perceives himself will influence his behaviour and his grades – also his choice of male and female friends, schools, and career.

His view of himself, in short, influences every decision he will ever make.

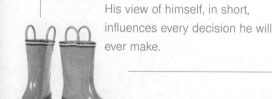

# A sense of self

Every word, action, and method of child-training you now employ either builds or destroys your child's self-image.

Self-respect is basic.

The mental picture we have of ourselves is formed by feedback accumulated from others over the years and through the experiences of life.

# Self-respect *is* important

People who possess self-respect like themselves, have confidence in their abilities, and are satisfied with their life and work. Since they have confidence in their abilities, they are able to risk attempting new things. If they encounter failures, they have the ability to deal with them without whipping themselves mercilessly with guilt.

# Get out of
# the rut of failure

Everyone can move out of the failure pattern
and begin afresh. Those with self-respect
not only feel innate value, but they also
know they have an important contribution
to make in life. They feel loved and, therefore,
can genuinely love others. Because they
feel good about themselves they are able
to respond positively to people and life
situations.

# Positive people

Those with a good self-concept are free to throw their energies into solving problems rather than fainting under their weight. They can accept the value of their accomplishments without becoming conceited. They feel equal to others and able to measure up to others' positive opinions of them.

# Bragging
# and boasting

Self-respect is not egotistical. In fact, bragging and boasting about oneself and one's accomplishments are classic symptoms of low self-worth.

That is true of parents and children.

# Few things are more important than self-respect

History tells us of many intelligent and gifted individuals who've become alcoholics, drug addicts, or suicide victims in order to escape from a self they grew to loathe.

# How negative feelings originate

It all begins in the tender years of childhood. Most parents cannot stop with a plain NO to a child when his behaviour infringes the rights of others. The typical parent feels he must continue: 'No, you naughty child. That's just nasty.' Words such as bad, slow, ugly, stupid, naughty, ridiculous, clumsy and thick downgrade a child's feelings of worth.

# Beware of putdowns

Subjected to a constant barrage of putdowns, along with a non-verbal disrespect or emotional neglect, a child begins to grow up feeling ashamed of, and dissatisfied with, himself.

# Competition

Unfortunately the structure of society is designed to promote feelings of inadequacy. Competition to be 'the best' permeates every classroom. Awards and rewards go to the winners of sports and other activities. Prizes await the champions. Fierce competition for popularity dominates the teen years.

# Winners and losers

Wherever there are winners there must be losers. Those who play the game and lose feel the pains of unacceptance and inferiority. Belittling remarks at home, added to the competition-packed society, set the stage for a child to belittle and refuse to accept himself.

# Build it from birth

Children catch the signals that build or destroy self-worth – almost from birth.

Parents fail to render support needed for feelings of adequacy to develop during the tender years. This has the potential of initiating a lifetime of self-castigation, self-recrimination, and self-unaccountability.

Such feelings begin during the formative years and are nurtured by a performance-orientated society.

# Dimensions of self-respect

By the time the child blows out that one little candle on his first birthday cake, his self-respect is already vulnerable. When an infant is only a few months old, he can distinguish between censure and praise.

His awareness of parental love and respect lays the crucial foundation for his self-respect.

# Infancy

As a child nears his third or fourth birthday, his world widens to include a community of people. Nursery, pre-school, or day-care classes, attendance at school, television viewing, and listening to books being read increases his exposure to others. By the time he turns 7 or 8, when his social life enlarges again, a child may already be wrestling with feelings of inferiority.

# Self-respect must be learned

A child is not born feeling good about himself. Although tendencies to either positive or negative feelings about oneself may be inherent, self-respect generally evolves from a child's daily interactions with others.

# Positive experiences

The more positive experiences you provide
for your child and the more positive the
feedback he receives from you, then the
greater the chances that he will learn that
he is a person of worth and adequacy.

# Self-respect must be learned

Wealth and possessions can be inherited,
but feelings of self-respect are learned.

Spoken or unspoken, 'How am I doing?'
lurks in every child's subconscious mind.

# Developing skills

Few things are better for developing a child's
sense of adequacy as the development of
skills or, possibly, a 'speciality'.

Carrying out household chores and duties
in a responsible manner also contributes to
a child's positive feelings about himself.

# Self-respect must be experienced

If a child doesn't feel your warmth and acceptance, your words will not convince him, no matter how many times you repeat yourself.

*Your actions must reinforce your words.*

# Loving your child is not enough

You must *feel* your acceptance of him as a person – *feel* your appreciation of his individual worth whether or not he accomplishes anything great in life.

Love is not the greatest gift parents can give to a child – self-respect is.

# Early training

*'Too much importance cannot be placed upon the early training of children. The lessons learned, the habits formed, during the years of infancy and childhood, have more to do with the formation of the character and the direction of the life than have all the instruction and training of after years.'*
Ministry of Healing, page 380

# A child is not capable of experiencing or returning love until he first learns to respect himself.

Three feelings that a child senses significantly affect his comprehension of self-worth:

Uniqueness
Belonging
Human love.

# Uniqueness

Every child must know that he is unique, special and deserves respect.

This uniqueness can be found by being the oldest, middle or youngest child, or through a special talent or ability.

Recognise in each of your children the uniqueness he brings to your family.

# Belonging

A child's sense of belonging derives from his sense of whether Mum and Dad are happy when he is around.

The child who feels that he is an unnecessary addition or believes that he is an 'unhappy accident' will have a difficult time feeling respected.

# Part of the group

We all have a basic need to be 'a part of' or 'in with' a group. A child is no different. He needs to experience a 'we' feeling in his family. Such a feeling is fundamentally established in infancy. From that he establishes a basic trust in people.

# Human love

It is vital that your child remains special and dear to you even if you don't approve of all he does.

A child needs to be certain he is loved. Nothing you say should give the impression that love is conditional on good behaviour.

# Because
# he is yours

Love your child because he is yours. You
must love little Johnny, not because he is
behaving right now, not because he gets
good marks at school, not because he's
good at sports, not because he's an obedient
child,

*but because he is yours.*

**Too many parents evaluate the worth of their child by his ability to make them look good.**

Good looks and intelligence are undoubtedly a plus, but love is not conditional upon them.

# Slow learners

Parents of slow learners should de-emphasise the importance of academic achievement and focus instead on the child's strengths and good qualities. In the light of eternity there are more important things in life than school reports with straight A's. Children should be helped to develop a speciality, a talent, or particular skill to compensate for their weaknesses.

# False values

A child who lacks average mental ability may find himself caught in a whirlpool of depression – the wasted victim of another false value created by our society.

The worth of an individual must not be measured by his Intelligence Quotient.

# Money important?

Financial deprivation can seriously handicap a youngster's peer acceptance, particularly if his clothing does not fall within acceptable norms. A child from a poor family or from a family whose parents are unaware of peer pressure to conform through dress could become a social outcast.

# 'All you need is love'?

People often naively assert that all a child needs is love and he will develop satisfactorily. No! Love is not enough! You may be able to control factors inside the home, but you cannot control the world outside your home. Your child must be able to function adequately in spite of the problems life has dealt him.

# Preparation, not protection

Our job as parents is not to protect our children from every hurt in life, but rather to prepare our children to accept the inevitable hurts and nobly rise above them. In other words, we can teach our children how to cope with the false values that stem from our society.

# Your example

Your example will mean a lot. If you can
laugh at your own shortcomings and
mistakes, this will go a long way in helping
your child over some of the rough spots of
life. Teach your child to remember his
failures with a smile.

# Self-deprecation

Constant self-deprecation on the part of the parent can become a bad habit that is difficult to break. Those with low self-esteem commonly love to recite their own inadequacies. By doing so they frequently pass them on to their children.

## Road blocks
## to self-respect

Yelling, screaming,
and constant criticism
tell a child that you do
not love him or care
about his feelings.

# Finding fault

Parents with low self-esteem particularly have a compulsive need to find fault with everything a child does. Soon the child feels that it is impossible to please this parent or to measure up to his expectations.

Be determined to catch your children doing something right!

# Spoken or unspoken

Whether spoken or unspoken, criticism is by far the most common and destructive cause of low self-esteem. Feelings of unacceptance do not always have to be verbalised to be experienced. A lack of appreciation or recognition speaks as loudly to a child as if it were verbally announced.

# Authoritarian parents?

An adult's domineering or bossy attitude implies to the child that he isn't capable of completing an assigned task unless his parent is there to supervise.

Authoritarian parents weaken self-worth. The child who is constantly told what to do develops few inner controls and lacks faith in his own abilities to carry out tasks for himself.

# Over-protective?

Over-protectiveness or excessive sheltering
can also make a child feel rejected because
he never has an opportunity to make
decisions for himself.

A mother who fights all the neighbourhood
battles in order to protect her 'precious' from
the cruel world inhibits his progress towards
a positive self-image.

# Quality time

Parents are advised to spend more time with the child, yet it is not *quantity*, but *quality* time that is important.

A father who spends hours with his boys doing projects and games but only seeks to put them down or play them off against one another is doing them no favours.

# Be interested!

Some parents show rejection through lack of interest. It's as if they have said, 'Don't bother me with your troubles. I've got troubles enough of my own. Hurry and grow up and get out of here.'

Some of the most crippling effects arise from parents who don't have time or who have been emotionally handicapped themselves by unloving relationships.

# Cause for joy

*The father of godly children has cause for joy. What a pleasure to have children who are wise.*
Proverbs 23:24, NLT

Parents who are happy with themselves can tolerate a lot of misbehaviour from their children.

# Those first years

'It is during the first years of a child's life that his mind is most susceptible to impressions either good or evil. During these years decided progress is made in either a right direction or a wrong one.

'Too much importance cannot be placed on the early training of children. The lessons that a child learns during the first seven years of life have more to do with forming his character than all that it learns in future years.'
Child Guidance, page 193

# Catch them young?

*'Many neglect their duty during the first years of their children's lives, thinking that when they get older, they will then be very careful to repress wrong and educate them in the right. But the very time for them to do this work is when the children are babes in their arms . . . A firm, decided, straightforward course of action will be productive of the best results.'*
Child Guidance, page194

# Is anyone watching?

Our accepting and rejecting attitudes depend on where we are and who is watching – the old double standard. Most of us tend to be less accepting at a friend's home, in a restaurant, at church – anywhere our child's public behaviour reflects back on us.

Children notice inconsistency.

# Unconditional love

The key is the ability to accept the child at all times, while perhaps not accepting everything he does. Just as God hates sin and loves the sinner, so parents should differentiate between the child's behaviour and the child himself if they want him to build a positive self-image.

# Don't discourage

*Children, always obey your parents, for this pleases the Lord. Fathers, do not aggravate your children, or they will become discouraged.*
Colossians 3:20, 21, NLT

We love our children deeply, we care for them, we even give our lives for them. And yet in the day-to-day struggle for existence some of our love gets lost.

# God's special love

*'Those who love God should feel deeply interested in the children and youth. To them God can reveal his truth and salvation. Jesus calls the little ones who believe on him the lambs of his flock. He has a special love for and interest in children. . . . The most precious offering that the children can give to Jesus is the freshness of their childhood.'*
Reflecting Christ, page 373

# Roots of wrong attitudes

What reasons may lie behind the rejection
of the child? Many a child feels rejection
because he is told 'He came at the wrong
time' or she is told 'We really wanted a boy.'
Some couples are so emotionally immature
that they are totally unprepared for the
responsibility of parenthood. Still other
parents have unrealistic expectations of
their children, expectations that their
children can never live up to.

# Peer pressure

Parents are not the only ones who affect a child's self-respect. Any person who spends long periods of time with him helps to determine his self-image. This person may be a relative, neighbour, babysitter, brother or sister. Teachers have a marked influence over a child because of their constant association.

# Countering peer pressure

The more acceptance
a child experiences
within the family,
the more rejection
he can withstand
from outside.

# Does your child suffer from low self-worth?

Here are some of the symptoms: lacks decision-making ability, retreats into a world of fantasy, repeated deliberate misbehaviour, abnormal attempts to please, habitual crying, tension, puts self and others down.

Before you take an inventory, remember 'normal behaviour' can vary widely!

# A cry for help?

The worse a child's behaviour, the greater his cry for approval. The more your child misbehaves, the more trying, withdrawn or obnoxious he is – the more starved he is for attention and acceptance. The greater the defences, the withdrawal or misbehaviour, the greater the need.

# Self-concepts can change

A child's self-concept is not forged for all time, although once established it is not easily disturbed.

The child who is convinced that he is no good believes only messages that confirm his feeling.

# Self-worth
# is learned

Since feelings of worth are
learned,
earned
and experienced,
rather than inherited, attitudes towards
the self can change when one encounters
a positive experience with people and life.

# Strategies for building self-worth

If you have had problems accepting your child, confess it to the child. Identify the cause. Ask your child's forgiveness. Ask God's forgiveness.

Recognise that your child is a special gift to you and that God has a special purpose for him.

# Express verbal acceptance of your child daily

If your child has issues help him to develop a 'speciality', a special interest or talent.

# The rejected child

Perhaps your child is suffering from rejection at school.

Encourage him to express his hurt to you. Use active listening skills.

The freer your child feels to express himself, the more likely you will be able to discover the real source of the problem.

# Special skills

If your child is overly sensitive, it signals
low self-esteem. Work with him to develop
special skills that can act as a compensating
factor when he receives rejection.

Teach him to cope, rather than mope!

# Happiness is feeling good about yourself

You provide a role model for your child, who quickly senses any lack of self-worth you might demonstrate. If you have low feelings of worth, they will in all likelihood contaminate your offspring like a deadly virus.

# You can make it!

By God's grace it is possible to
re-programme a defective self-image.
God gives you the power to carry out his
purpose and image in you as you behold
him – in his Word.

# Give it to God

One girl found it difficult to achieve high
grades in school. Turning her low self-image
over to God, each day she would repeat to
herself these transforming words:

*I can do all things through Christ who
strengthens me.*
Philippians 4:13, NKJV

# Your greatest gift to your child

Happiness is feeling good about oneself, and the greatest gift you can give your child is a healthy self-respect. The word love can now be profoundly understood. This is the firm foundation for homemade happiness. Indeed, this is truly living!

# Neglected children

*'How interestedly the Lord Jesus knocks at the door of families where there are little children to be educated and trained! ...'*
That I May Know Him, page 39

# An act of love

It is an act of love to accept another person
just as he is, for to feel accepted means to
feel loved. Feeling loved promotes growth
of mind and body and is an effective
therapeutic force in repairing psychological
and physical damage.

# Communicating acceptance

Many times the lines of communication between parent and child are severed because the child detects feelings of rejection. It is not enough for a parent to *feel* accepting. He must be able to convey these feelings of acceptance in terms the child can readily understand.

# Don't interrupt!

Non-interference – another method of showing acceptance – can be shown a child by allowing him to play or participate in activities without interruption. To interrupt a child, to give instructions, to make suggestions, or to offer assistance while he is engaged in an activity reveals your lack of trust in the child's abilities.

# Interested listening

Passive, interested listening can also communicate acceptance. The difference between passive listening and active listening centres in what you listen for. Passive listening simply means that as you listen for information you communicate your acceptance by saying nothing or very little. . . . No comments of judgement are conveyed, only acceptance.

# Passive listening is a skill few parents have mastered

They seem to feel it their duty to correct, refute, admonish, restate or reinterpret everything their child says to them.

As a child is allowed to express his feelings in an atmosphere of acceptance he can more easily move towards solving problems on his own initiative.

# Prepare to be threatened!

Parents who want open communication with their youngster must prepare themselves to hear some pretty threatening things. What good are you as a listener if you will hear only the good? Young people need to share their joys, yes, but they also need someone with whom they can share their problems.

# Corrective

*My children, listen when your father corrects
you. Pay attention and learn good judgement.*
Proverbs 4:1, NLT

*Don't fail to discipline your children.*
Proverbs 23:13, NLT

*To discipline a child produces wisdom,
but a mother is disgraced by an
undisciplined child.*
Proverbs 29:15, NLT

# Releasing intense feelings

Most parents do not know how to release their own negative feelings or how to help their children channel their intense feelings.

Often when children share emotions with us, we proceed to tell them how they should or should not feel – as though our statements of logic can erase their feelings!

# The fastest way

The fastest way to get rid of negative emotions is to express them. If we repress them, they can form bitterness.

A little boy said, 'My daddy made me sit down, but I'm standing up inside.' By telling children to calm down, not to be angry, or to stop the feeling, we push them from us.

# Active listening

Invitations to communicate open the door for mutual understanding, but parents need to know how to keep the door open. Active listening is an excellent skill for this purpose. Not only is information gleaned by active listening but, more importantly, the true feelings behind the words of the child become discernible.

# Get into the root of the problem

The parent should listen for the meaning behind the problem (the feelings) and then restate the feeling so there is no misunderstanding of the meaning.

As your child moves deeper and deeper into the problem he is experiencing you must restrain the impulse to solve his problem or tell him what to do.

# Active listening does five specific things:

1. It helps the child learn how to handle negative feelings.
2. It provides the basis for a close relationship between parent and child.
3. It helps a child move towards independent problem-solving.
4. It teaches a child to listen to a parent and to others.
5. It encourages a child to think for himself.

# 'He never listens!'

If you feel that your child never listens to what you say, it might be that you are 'modelling' this behaviour to him.

It is our duty as parents, however, to equip our child with the ability to deal with and solve the problems of life.

# Acceptance

The key word in active listening is acceptance. Acceptance of your child's feelings, ideas, or opinions, in spite of how different they might be from how you want your child to respond to life.

# Listen to your child . . .

. . . He is a small human being filled
with wonder and curiosity and eagerness.
Listen to his voice with your ears and
eyes and heart.

# Re-evaluation

Something may happen to you when you practise active listening. Your own attitudes or opinions may change as you really understand accurately how another feels. Opening yourself to the experiences of others invites the possibility of re-evaluating your own experiences. And this can be scary, because a defensive person cannot afford to expose himself to ideas and views that differ from his own.

# Home –
# a place of sharing

Make your home a place for sharing ideas
and thoughts without fear of humiliation and
ridicule. Your children will start bringing up all
kinds of problems that they never discussed
with you before, and home will become a
place for growth.

# Time to talk

Communication is a two-way street. Both parents and child need to send. But the timing is important. If listening doesn't settle the matter, then talk. But sending a message when a child is in an emotional upheaval simulates someone trying to put up wallpaper in a room full of steam.

Your child can't hear you when he is churning with emotion.

# 'Parent deafness'

Telling children what to do creates 'parent deafness'. Children resent it when they are told what they must or should do. This kind of communication sets up roadblocks to effective communication and implies that you don't think the child is capable of initiating good behaviour on his own.

# Putting it across effectively

Choose words carefully. Choose *suitable* words to let the child know that parents have feelings, too. If you could simply tell your child how his unacceptable behaviour makes you feel, it would be what is referred to as an I-statement. 'I really get upset when I find your chores have not been done.'

# I-statements

An I-statement has three parts:
1. A statement of how the child's unacceptable behaviour makes you feel.
2. A non-blameful description of the child's behaviour (it is acceptable to use the word *you* in this description).
3. An explanation regarding the tangible effect of that behaviour on you.

# Annoying behaviour

I-statements contain an explanation of how the parent *feels* about the annoying behaviour. They do not condemn the child, but refer only to the youngster's unacceptable behaviour, differentiating between the child and his behaviour.

# In place
# of nagging

Over a period of time, I-statements can do
more to encourage a child to change his
unacceptable behaviour – without damaging
his self-respect or hurting a relationship –
than all the rewards, punishments or nagging
most parents have unsuccessfully used.

# Use the volume switch!

Arnold Bennett said that when you talk to someone else, you actually speak twice: once through what you say, and again in the way you say it. He states that 90% of the friction in life is caused by the tone of voice used.

# Don't let it fester!

Don't let your child keep his anger with you buried inside to fester and erupt in later years. The scriptural admonition, *'Let not the sun go down upon your wrath'* (Ephesians 4:26, KJV), holds for children and parents.

Heal the wounds while they are scratches and easy to mend.

# Discipline

The word discipline is related to the word
*disciple*. Plus, when you discipline your child,
you are really training him to be a disciple or
learner of you, his teacher.

# Respect!

If a child feels respected when his parents
correct him, he will not lose respect for
himself even though he may have done
something very wrong.

Never should discipline destroy self-respect.

# Self-government

The object of discipline is the training of the child for self-government. A parent's ultimate goal in disciplining a child is to help him become a self-regulating person.

# The first year

Experts in childcare agree that, excluding the all-important prenatal period, the first year of life is ordinarily the most important one. Furthermore, the first month of the first year is the most important month, and each successive month is important to a lesser degree than the one that preceded it.

# Manipulation

Even an infant knows whether he can manipulate his parents, and if he can he will. If an infant is not taught to conform to a schedule that fits into the family routine by the time he is six months old, he will train his parents to fit into his schedule!

# Gain and maintain respect

That is the first avenue to discipline.
Respect, however, is a two-way street.
A mother should not expect respect from
Jimmy if she doesn't respect him.

Parents who gain and maintain their child's
respect during early years will have his
respect during teenage years.

# Respect, obedience, reverence

The most important lessons learned in the home are not reading, writing and arithmetic . . . but respect, obedience, reverence and self-control.

These must be taught patiently, tenderly, lovingly and consistently every day so as to become a part of the child's character for the rest of his life.

# Set limits

In order to maintain friendly relations,
it is necessary to establish well-defined
boundaries whenever two lives cross.
Your child needs to know what you will
permit and what you will prohibit.

# Teach reason and obedience

The long-range goal of parents is to teach a child to guide his own behaviour, to make good decisions, to reason clearly about choices, to solve problems on his own, and to plan ahead.

# Give reasons

When disciplining a child, tell him what he did right, what he did wrong, and why he is being punished.

After your child has been given examples of reasons for correct behaviour and for punishment, begin to ask him to state the reasons.

# Rules

The rules we make should be short, easy to remember, and stated positively.

Children hear too many 'don'ts'.

A home with the best discipline and the fewest disciplinary problems will be a home with a few simple rules.

# Speak once; then act

But always balance love and control. Don't be an authoritarian parent. And don't be a permissive parent. Above all, don't be an unloving parent.

# Emotional starvation

Emotional starvation is as dangerous
as physical starvation.

There is only one subtle kind of rejection
that disturbs professionals more than
emotional starvation: using severe
punishment, constantly criticising or
nagging a child, seeing only his
shortcomings, holding a child to
unsuitable or unattainable standards.

# Step aside!

It is difficult to step aside when you feel
your partner as a parent is not handling a
disciplinary situation correctly. But stepping
aside is exactly what you should do! Far
greater damage is done to the child if he
observes both of you disagreeing over
how he should be handled.

# Avoid extremes

A child needs discipline in an atmosphere of love, and competent parents avoid extremes in either love or punishment.

If you love your child with a nurturing love, then you can discipline him with the proper balance between love and control.

# Motives

Every time your child disobeys you must
take your brain off automatic pilot and
ascertain the child's motives.

We do not want to punish a child for being
a child.

# Spanking

Parents hesitate to admit it, but the main purpose in spanking a child is to relieve their feelings of frustration. And almost every parent who has ever lived has become frustrated by certain disruptive behaviours, become angry, lost his temper, and a swift spanking was the result. This may relieve the parent's frustration, but what of the child?

# Parent popularity

It takes real character on the part of parents to teach obedience, because a child is not always in harmony with parental decisions. But parents cannot take a popularity poll every week to see how they are doing in the eyes of the child. Parents are not running for office. They hold an office, and it is their duty to fill that office.

# Forgiveness

We should tenderly forgive when a child
confesses disobedience. Little feet are easily
led astray. Little tongues wander naturally
from the truth. Little hands find many things
to get into. Let us not forget that in requiring
obedience, loving mothers and fathers teach
mercy and kindness.

# Personality
# and character

Personality refers only to 'outward behaviour'.
Character refers to moral excellence.

The word *character* comes from the Greek
word meaning 'engrave'.

All the attitudes and facets that go into
shaping a child's character are *learned* –
most of them from you.

# The early years

During the early years of life, character development is most rapid and inherently most susceptible to guidance.

Let every Christian father and mother realise that when their child is 3 years old they have already done more than half of all they will ever do for his character. Studies indicate that the first five or six years are the most formative period.

# Mutual parental respect

The atmosphere of the home is particularly important to the child's budding development. If the parents do not respect one another, if they quarrel all the time or are jealous or untruthful, if they engage in power struggles of any kind, their child will suffer from distortion of development – regardless of how carefully they try to hide their own problems.

# The main ingredient

The main ingredient for a child's character development is that the parents relate to each other with mutual love, respect and appreciation. As surely as a mirror, the child will reflect the same character traits to which it is continually exposed.

# Inner controls

Before a youngster leaves childhood he is
expected to have developed inner controls
that will help him make proper choices.

As the child grows, the parent should
gradually shift away from heavy external
controls so that the child can develop
internal controls.

# Take time

Take time for a hand-in-hand nature walk, and answer your child's questions about God's creation. Take time to build a kite, and savour the delight of your child's face as he watches it race and dance on the wings of the wind. Take time to listen to your child *now*, for tomorrow he may not wish to talk with you.

SLOW DOWN, CHRISTIAN MOTHER. SLOW DOWN, CHRISTIAN FATHER.

Take time for the important things now. Sort through your priorities. God will bless and honour your efforts.